Rubber Band Loom Fun!

LEISURE ARTS, INC.
Maumelle, Arkansas

EDITORIAL STAFF

Vice President of Editorial: Susan White Sullivan

Creative Art Director: Katherine Laughlin

Publications Director: Leah Lampirez

Craft Design Director: Patti Wallenfang

Special Projects Director: Susan Frantz Wiles

Technical Editor: Mary Sullivan Hutcheson

Contributing Editor: Jean Lewis

Designer: Kelly Reider

Art Category Manager: Lora Puls

Graphic Artist: Jessica Bramlett

Prepress Technician: Stephanie Johnson

Contributing Photographers: Jason Masters and Ken West

Contributing Photo Stylist: Lori Wenger

BUSINESS STAFF

President and Chief Executive Officer: Rick Barton

Senior Vice President of Operations: Jim Dittrich

Vice President of Finance: Fred F. Pruss

Vice President of Sales-Retail Books: Martha Adams

Vice President of Mass Market: Bob Bewighouse

Vice President of Technology and Planning:
   Laticia Mull Dittrich

Controller: Tiffany P. Childers

Information Technology Director: Brian Roden

Director of E-Commerce: Mark Hawkins

Manager of E-Commerce: Robert Young

Retail Customer Service Manager: Stan Raynor

ISBN-13: 978-1-4647-1578-5

Contents

Rubber band jewelry is taking the world by storm! Everybody wants the colorful bracelets, necklaces, and rings that are so much fun to create on looms with rows of plastic pins. Whether it's called Rainbow Loom®, Wonder Loom™, FunLoom™, Cra-Z-Loom™, or other names, the looms and their supplies create a shopping frenzy each time a new shipment arrives at stores.

Getting Started

Just like the looms, there are lots of types of bands and clips to choose from. We show a C-shaped clip to join the bracelets, but you may have another shape; either will work. You could even use ribbon, cord, or embroidery floss in place of the clip to dress up your creations.

Each project in this book will have a Chart to show where to place the bands, as well as illustrations to show looping the bands.

To the right is a blank Chart like the ones that will show band placement. Each ∪ shape represents a loom pin.

The band's color & direction will be shown on the Chart & illustrations. It's very important to follow the Steps when placing & looping the bands on the loom pins.

On the illustrations, the band that you are working with is shown in color. Bands that are in the background or not being used for that Step are shown in a much lighter color.

Let's get started with a basic Single Bracelet in red & aqua where you'll learn to place & loop the bands.

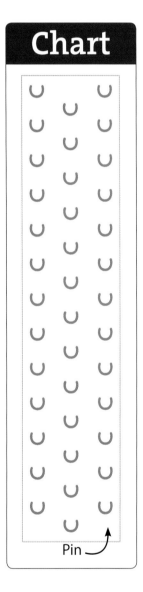

Chart

Pin

Chart

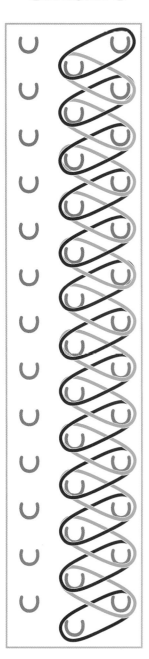

Single

Band Placement

!
When
Placing
the Bands:
Place the loom on the table with the open parts of the pins facing away from you. This bracelet only uses 2 rows of pins.

Step 1:

Use your fingers to place a red band on the loom. Push it down on the pins.

Step 2:

Then add an aqua band & push it down on the pins.

Step 3:

Continue to place red & aqua bands on the loom pins until you reach the top of the loom (see the Chart on the left).

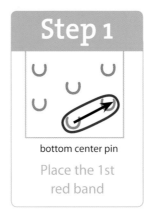

Step 1

bottom center pin

Place the 1st red band

Step 2

Place the 1st aqua band

Single continued on page 8.

Looping

> **!**
> **When Looping the Bands:**
>
> • Turn the loom around so the open parts of the pins are facing you.
>
> • Always use the looping tool to pick up & loop the bands.

Step 1:

Use the looping tool to go down into the center pin hole. Move the red band out of the way & grab the aqua band with the hook. Pull it up & off the pin.

Step 1

Grab the aqua band on the center pin

Step 2

Loop the aqua band to the left pin

Step 2:

Keeping the band on the hook, loop the aqua band over the pin to the left; remove the hook.

Step 3:

Go down into the next pin hole on the left & pick up the red band. Pull it up & off the pin.

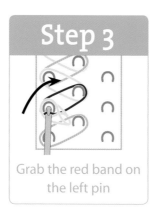

Step 3

Grab the red band on the left pin

Step 4

Loop the red band to the center pin

Step 4:

Loop the red band over to the center pin.

Step 5:

Continue picking up & looping the red & aqua bands until you've looped the last red band.

Step 6:

Slide a C-clip over the red band loops.

Step 6

Slide a C-clip on the red band loops

Step 7:

Carefully pull all the bands from the pins.

Step 8:

Join the bracelet by slipping the C-clip through the loop at the beginning of the bracelet.

Congratulations! You've just made your first rubber band bracelet! Make several of these in different colors to practice working with the loom & looping tool. You can also make a ring to match your bracelet using 9-10 bands.

Chart

Triple Single

Band Placement

The illustrations show the rainbow version of the bracelet.
The stripes are formed by straight lines of elastic bands; the base under
the stripes is formed by bands that are placed on the pins in triangles.

! When Placing the Bands:	• Place the loom on the table with the open parts of the pins facing away from you.
	• Use your fingers to place the bands on the loom.
	• Follow the Steps when placing the bands.
	• Push each band down after you place it on the pins.

Steps 1-3:

Place bands on each pin row, starting with yellow & referring to the photo on page 10 for color sequence.

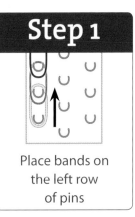

Step 1

Place bands on the left row of pins

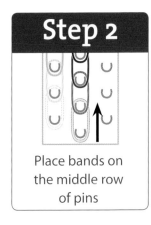

Step 2

Place bands on the middle row of pins

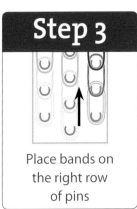

Step 3

Place bands on the right row of pins

Step 4:

Place white bands (shown in grey) in triangles (see the Chart on page 10).

Triple Single continued on page 12.

Looping

> **!**
> **When Looping the Bands:**
> - Turn the loom around so the open parts of the pins are facing you.
> - Always use the looping tool to pick up & loop the bands.

Step 1
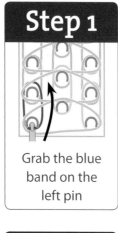

Grab the blue band on the left pin

Step 2
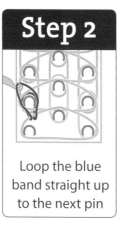

Loop the blue band straight up to the next pin

Step 3
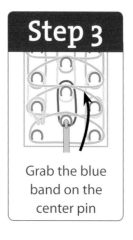

Grab the blue band on the center pin

Step 4
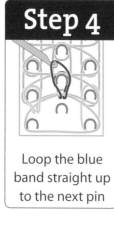

Loop the blue band straight up to the next pin

Step 5
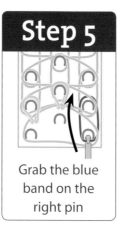

Grab the blue band on the right pin

Step 6
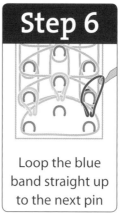

Loop the blue band straight up to the next pin

Step 7: Continue picking up & looping the bands until you reach the top of the loom. Finish the bracelet with a white extension & C-clip (see pages 47-48).

Tips: Our color combos (see above) include red, white, & blue stripes with a white base & extension, blue, green, & aqua stripes with a black base & extension, & aqua, green, & purple stripes with a yellow base & extension. A bracelet without an extension looks great on a spring-closure barrette; just tie the end loops to the barrette ends.

Fishtail

Band Placement

The illustrations show the rainbow version of the bracelet.
This four-sided bracelet is made on just 2 side-by-side loom pins.

> **!**
> **When Placing the Bands:**
>
> • Place the loom on the table with the open parts of the pins facing left.
> • Use your fingers to place the bands on the loom.
> • Follow the Steps when placing the bands.
> • Push each band down after you place it on the pins.

Step 1

Twist a yellow band into a figure 8 & place it on the pins

Step 2

Place a pink band on top the yellow band

Step 3

Place a red band on top the pink band

***Fishtail** continued on page 16.*

Looping

> **!**
> **When Looping the Bands:**
> • Always use the looping tool to pick up & loop the bands.

Step 1

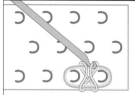

Grab the yellow band on the left pin

Step 2

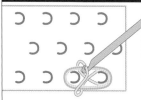

Loop the band to the center over the pink & red bands

Step 3

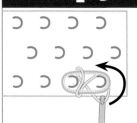

Grab the yellow band on the right pin

Step 4

Loop the band to the center over the pink & red bands

Step 5

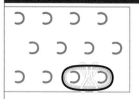

Place a purple band on the pins

Step 6

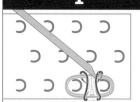

Loop the pink band to the center

Step 7

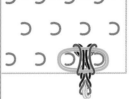

Place a blue band on the pins

Step 8

Continue looping the bottom band to the center

Step 8:

Continue looping the bottom band to the center & placing a new band on the pins (referring to the photo on page 14 for color sequence). The bracelet will extend between the 2 pins.

Step 9:

When the bracelet is long enough, loop the bottom band to center.

Step 10

Grab the last band from the pins & slide it on the looping tool

Step 11

Slide a C-clip on the band loops at the beginning & end to join

Color Tips: The other color combinations (shown on page 15) are easy to make! For two colors, alternate the colors on the pins & to make three colors, just repeat the color sequence.

Chart

Diamond

Band Placement

The illustrations show the blue & aqua version of the bracelet.

This bracelet looks great with 2 colors.

> **!**
> **When Placing the Bands:**
>
> - Place the loom on the table with the open parts of the pins facing away from you.
> - Use your fingers to place the bands on the loom.
> - Follow the Steps when placing the bands.
> - Push each band down after you place it on the pins.

Step 1

Place the 1st aqua band

Step 2

Place the 2nd aqua band

Diamond *continued on page 20.*

Step 3

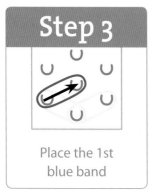

Place the 1st
blue band

Step 4

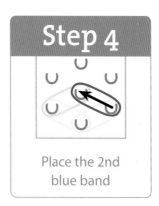

Place the 2nd
blue band

Step 5:

Ending with 1 aqua band at the top, continue to
place the aqua & blue bands on the loom pins
until you reach the top of the loom (see the Chart
on page 18).

Looping

!
When Looping the Bands:
- Turn the loom around so the open parts of the pins are facing you.
- Always use the looping tool to pick up & loop the bands.

Step 1

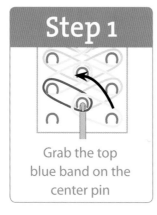

Grab the top
blue band on the
center pin

Step 2

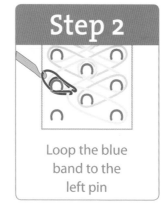

Loop the blue
band to the
left pin

Step 3

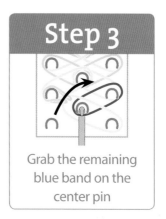

Grab the remaining
blue band on the
center pin

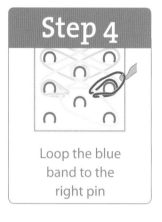

Step 4

Loop the blue
band to the
right pin

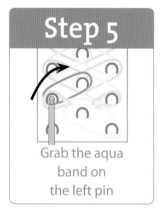

Step 5

Grab the aqua
band on
the left pin

Step 6

Loop the aqua
band to the
center pin

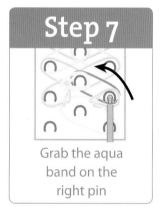

Step 7

Grab the aqua
band on the
right pin

Step 8

Loop the aqua
band to the
center pin

Step 9:

Continue picking up
& looping the aqua &
blue bands until you've
looped the last set of
bands.

Step 10:

Refer to Steps 5-9 on page 47 to pull a new aqua loop through the center pin
loops & to remove the bracelet from the loom. To finish the bracelet, refer to
Step 5, page 48, to join the ends with a C-clip.

Color Tips: Show off your favorite colors by combining dark green & brown, dark brown & lime green, purple & black, or orange & white.

Chart

Double Rhombus

Band Placement

The illustrations show the yellow & green version of the bracelet.
This 2 color bracelet forms a double rhombus with each set of elastic bands.

> **!**
> **When Placing the Bands:**
>
> - Place the loom on the table with the open parts of the pins facing away from you.
> - Use your fingers to place the bands on the loom.
> - Follow the Steps when placing the bands.
> - Push each band down after you place it on the pins.

Step 1

Place the 1st yellow band

Step 2

Place the 2nd yellow band

Step 3
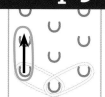
Place the 1st green band

Double Rhombus continued on page 26.

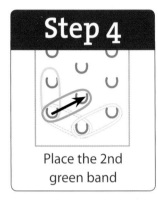

Step 4

Place the 2nd green band

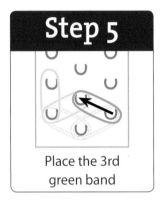

Step 5

Place the 3rd green band

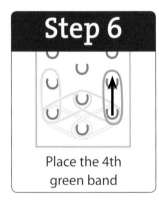

Step 6

Place the 4th green band

Step 7

Place the 5th green band

Step 8:

Beginning with yellow, repeat from Step 3 to continue placing green & yellow bands on the loom pins until you reach the top of the loom (see the Chart on page 24). The last set of bands will only have 4 yellow bands.

Looping

> **!**
> **When Looping the Bands:**
> - Turn the loom around so the open parts of the pins are facing you.
> - Always use the looping tool to pick up & loop the bands.

Step 1
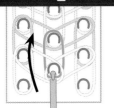
Grab the green band on the center pin

Step 2

Loop the green band straight up to the next pin

Step 3
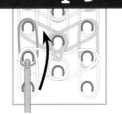
Grab the green band on the left pin

Step 4

Loop the green band straight up to the next pin

Step 5
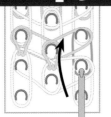
Grab the green band on the right pin

Step 6

Loop the green band straight up to the next pin

Step 7

Grab the top green band on the center pin

Double Rhombus continued on page 28.

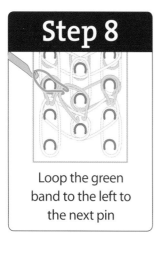

Step 8

Loop the green band to the left to the next pin

Step 9

Grab the remaining green band on the center pin

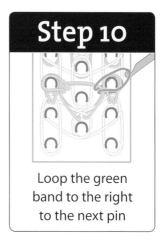

Step 10

Loop the green band to the right to the next pin

Step 11:

Continue picking up & looping the yellow & green bands until you reach the last 2 yellow bands. Pick up & loop the last 2 diagonal yellow bands to the center pin.

Step 12:

Refer to Steps 5-9 on page 47 & all of page 48 to finish the bracelet with a green extension & C-clip.

Color Tips: For other color combos (shown right), substitute blue for the green & aqua for the yellow or white for the green & pink for the yellow. For the rainbow bracelet, start with yellow bands; then add pink, red, purple, blue, aqua, & green bands.

Chart

Butterfly Blossoms

Band Placement

The illustrations show the pink, white, aqua, & purple version of the bracelet.
The "blossom body" is formed by the elastic bands placed in a hexagon shape;
the "butterfly wings" are formed by twisted bands placed on the loom.

! **When Placing the Bands:**	• Place the loom on the table with the open parts of the pins facing away from you.
	• Use your fingers to place the bands on the loom.
	• Follow the Steps when placing the bands.
	• Push each band down after you place it on the pins.

Step 1

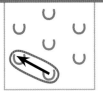

Place the 1st
pink band

Step 2

Place the 2nd
pink band

Butterfly Blossoms continued on page 32.

Step 3

Place the 3rd pink band

Step 4

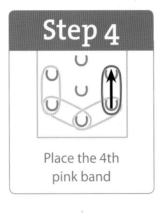

Place the 4th pink band

Step 5

Place the 5th pink band

Step 6

Place the 6th pink band, completing the hexagon

Step 7

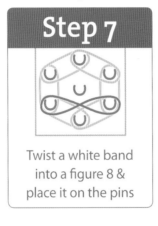

Twist a white band into a figure 8 & place it on the pins

Step 8

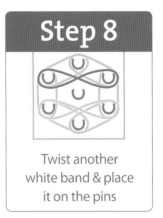

Twist another white band & place it on the pins

Step 9:

Repeat with 6 aqua bands & 2 purple bands. Continue to place the pink, white, aqua, & purple bands on the pins until you reach the top of the loom (see the Chart on page 30).

Tips: To make a pretty ring, attach a short (4-6 bands) extension (see pages 47-48) to a single blossom. For the headband, glue a five-blossom bracelet (without the extension) to a plain headband. Make a great necklace by adding cord or ribbon to the ends of three blossoms.

Butterfly Blossoms continued on page 34.

Looping

Step 1

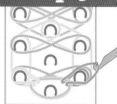

Place a doubled white band on the center pin

Step 2

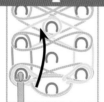

Grab the top aqua band on the center pin

Step 3

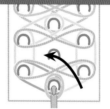

Loop the band to the left pin

Step 4

Grab the next aqua band on the center pin

Step 5

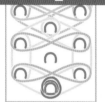

Loop the band to the right pin

Step 6

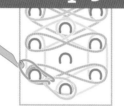

Grab the bottom aqua band on the left pin

Step 7

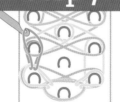

Loop the band straight up to the next pin

Step 8

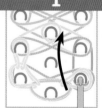

Grab the bottom aqua band on the right pin

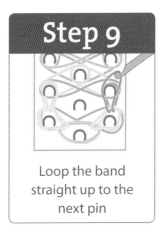

Step 9

Loop the band straight up to the next pin

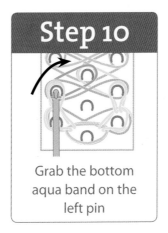

Step 10

Grab the bottom aqua band on the left pin

Step 11

Loop the band to the center pin

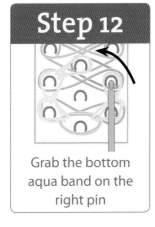

Step 12

Grab the bottom aqua band on the right pin

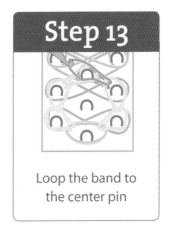

Step 13

Loop the band to the center pin

Step 14:

Continue picking up & looping the pink & aqua bands until you've looped the last blossom.

Step 15:

Refer to Steps 5-9 on page 47 & all of page 48 to finish the bracelet with a white extension & C-clip.

Chain Mail

Band Placement

The illustrations show the brown & orange version of the bracelet.
This bracelet is made on 4 loom pins.

> **!**
> **When Placing the Bands:**
>
> • Turn the loom so the open parts of the pins are facing to the right.
> • Use your fingers to place the bands on the loom.
> • Follow the Steps when placing the bands.
> • Push each band down after you place it on the pins.

Step 1

Twist brown bands into figure 8's & place on pins 1-4

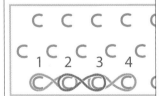

Step 2

Twist an orange band into a figure 8 & place it on pins 2 & 3

Chain Mail continued on page 38.

Looping

Step 1

Grab the brown band on pin 2

Step 2

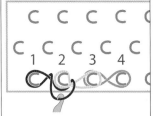

Loop the brown band to the front of pin 2

Step 3

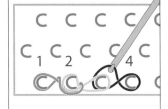

Grab the brown band on pin 3

Step 4

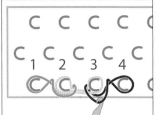

Loop the brown band to the front of pin 3

Step 5

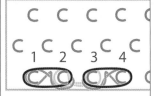

Place 2 more brown bands on pins 1-4

Step 6

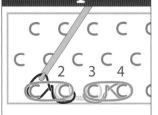

Grab the brown band on pin 1

Step 7

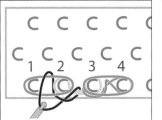

Loop the brown band to the front of pin 1

Step 8

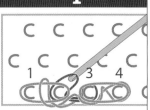

Grab the orange band on pin 2

Chain Mail *continued on page 40.*

Step 9

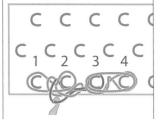

Loop the orange band to the front of pin 2

Step 10

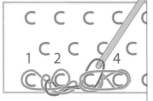

Grab the orange band on pin 3

Step 11

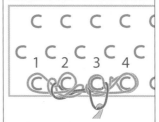

Loop the orange band to the front of pin 3

Step 12

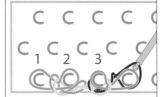

Grab the brown band on pin 4

Step 13

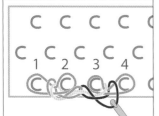

Loop the brown band to the front of pin 4

Step 14

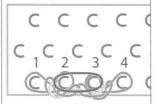

Place an orange band on pins 2 & 3

Step 15

Grab the brown band on pin 2

Step 16

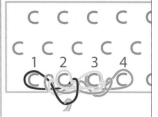

Loop the brown band to the front of pin 2

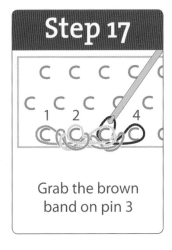

Step 17

Grab the brown band on pin 3

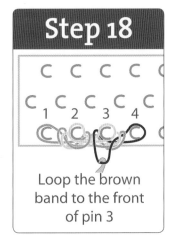

Step 18

Loop the brown band to the front of pin 3

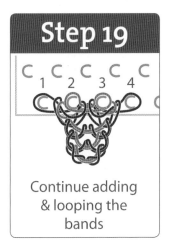

Step 19

Continue adding & looping the bands

Step 19:

Beginning with Step 5, continue adding & looping brown & orange bands. The bracelet will extend from the pins.

Step 20:

When the bracelet is long enough, loop the brown band on pin 1 to pin 2 & loop the brown band on pin 4 to pin 3.

Step 21:

Refer to Steps 5-8 on page 47 & Step 5 on page 48 to join the bracelet ends with a C-clip.

Tips: The Chain Mail bracelet looks great in all sorts of color combinations; try red & white or dark green & lime green. Our red & black bracelet is made on 6 pins instead of 4 – what an easy way to make a wider cuff!

Chart

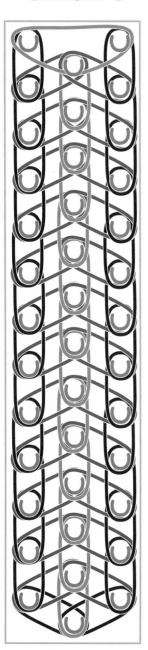

Zippy Chain

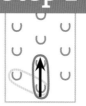

Band Placement

The illustrations show the red, white, & blue version of the bracelet.

This bracelet resembles a zipper & uses 3 band colors.

> **!**
> **When Placing the Bands:**
>
> • Place the loom on the table with the open parts of the pins facing away from you.
> • Use your fingers to place the bands on the loom.
> • Follow the Steps when placing the bands.
> • Push each band down after you place it on the pins.

Step 1	Step 2	Step 3
Place the 1st red band	Place a white band	Place the 2nd red band

Zippy Chain continued on page 44.

Step 4	Step 5	Step 6	Step 7
		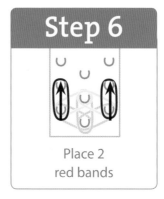	
Place the 1st blue band	Place 2nd blue band	Place 2 red bands	Place a white band

Step 8:

Moving up the loom & starting from Step 4, continue to place blue, red, & white bands on the loom pins until you reach the top of the loom (see the Chart on page 42). Place a white band in a triangle over the last 3 pins.

Color Tips: For our aqua, black, & blue combo shown on page 43, substitute aqua for the blue, black for the white, & blue for the red; for the white, gold, & dark brown combo, substitute white for the blue, gold for the white, & dark brown for the red. Or, make one in camo colors using brown for the blue, black for the white, & green for the red.

Looping

> **!** **When Looping the Bands:**
> - Turn the loom around so the open parts of the pins are facing you.
> - Always use the looping tool to pick up & loop the bands.

Step 1

Grab the top blue band on the center pin

Step 2

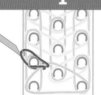

Loop the blue band to the left pin

Step 3

Grab the remaining blue band on the center pin

Step 4

Loop the blue band to the right pin

Step 5

Grab the white band on the center pin

Step 6

Loop the white band straight up to the next pin

Zippy Chain continued on page 46.

Step 7:

Continue picking up & looping the blue & white bands until you've looped the last white band.

Step 8:

Go back to the bottom of the loom & follow Steps 9-12 to pick up & loop the red bands until you've looped the last set of vertical red bands. Pick up & loop the last 2 diagonal red bands to the center pin.

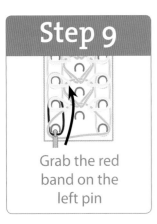

Step 9
Grab the red band on the left pin

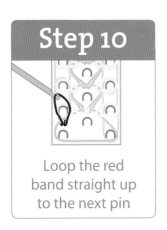

Step 10
Loop the red band straight up to the next pin

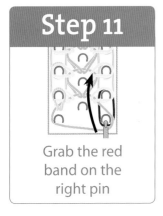

Step 11
Grab the red band on the right pin

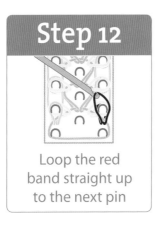

Step 12
Loop the red band straight up to the next pin

Step 13:

Refer to Steps 5-9 on page 47 & all of page 48 to finish the bracelet with a blue extension & C-clip.

Making a Bracelet Extension

Many bracelets need an extension to be long enough to wear; the project instructions will tell when to make one. The extension is also made on the loom pins. Follow Steps 1-9 to remove the bracelet from the loom.

Step 1
Grab the loops on the left pin

Step 2
Move the loops to the center pin

Step 3
Grab the loops on the right pin

Step 4
Move the loops to the center pin

Step 5
Grab all the loops on the center pin

Step 6
Pull a new band halfway through the loops

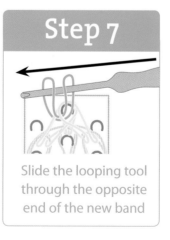

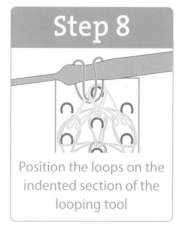

Step 7
Slide the looping tool through the opposite end of the new band

Step 8
Position the loops on the indented section of the looping tool

Step 9: Carefully remove the bracelet from the pins & set aside.

Making a Bracelet Extension continued on page 48.

Chart

Band Placement

> **!**
> **When Placing the Bands:**
> - Turn the loom so the open parts of the pins are facing away from you.
> - Starting at the loom bottom, use your fingers to place the bands on the loom (refer to your project instructions for band color & see the Chart on the left).
> - Push each band down after you place it on the pins.

Looping

> **!**
> **When Looping the Bands:**
> - Turn the loom around so the open parts of the pins are facing you.
> - Always use the looping tool to pick up & loop the bands.

Step 1

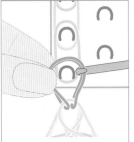

Transfer the bands on the looping tool to the bottom pin

Step 2

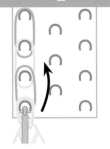

Grab the 1st extension band

Step 3

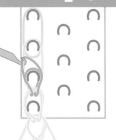

Loop the band straight up to the next pin

Step 4:

Continue picking up & looping the extension bands until you loop the last band.

Step 5

Slide a C-clip on the band loops

Step 6:

Pull the band with the C-clip off the pin. Carefully pull all the bands from the pins. Join the bracelet by slipping the C-clip through the loop (or loops) at the other end of the bracelet.